Divorce's Devastating Dilemmas

Navigating Complex Legal Procedures For Equitable Separation And Property Division

Isabelle Ashford

Contents

1 Chapter 1: Understanding Divorce

Divorce, the legal termination of a marriage, is a complex process varying significantly by jurisdiction. Understanding the foundational legal requirements is the crucial first step. Failing to grasp these fundamentals can lead to delays, increased costs, and ultimately, an unfavorable outcome.
Grounds for divorce, the legal reasons justifying the dissolution of a marriage, differ between states and countries. Some jurisdictions operate on a "no-fault" system, requiring only the assertion that the marriage is irretrievably broken. Others maintain "fault-based" grounds, demanding proof of specific marital misconduct such as adultery, cruelty, or abandonment. It's imperative to understand your state's specific laws to ensure your petition meets the required criteria. Careful research, or consultation with a legal professional, is vital in navigating this initial hurdle. The complexities involved often necessitate legal expertise to ensure the process is initiated correctly.
Residency requirements represent another critical aspect. Before filing for divorce, individuals must generally satisfy residency stipulations set by the court. These requirements specify the length

of time a person must reside within a particular jurisdiction before it will accept their petition. These periods can vary, ranging from a few weeks to several years. Meeting these requirements is non-negotiable; a failure to comply renders the petition inadmissible. This highlights the significance of understanding the jurisdictional rules prior to any action. Incorrectly initiating proceedings can lead to costly delays and necessitate restarting the entire process. Consider contacting legal representatives; they will provide clarity on all jurisdictional issues.

The legal and emotional implications of divorce are immense. The financial ramifications alone can be daunting. Assets and debts acquired during the marriage typically undergo division in accordance with equitable distribution principles. This process requires careful consideration of each asset's value, including real estate, personal property, and financial investments. Retirement accounts are frequently a contentious point, often demanding complex calculations and legal expertise to ensure a fair division. Debt allocation also forms a critical part of the process, impacting the financial future of both parties. Thorough understanding of the process, ideally with professional assistance, is crucial for a positive outcome.

Furthermore, custody arrangements for children—another highly emotional aspect of divorce—must be considered, often requiring intense negotiation or court intervention. Legal and physical custody, as two distinct concepts, must be thoroughly understood. Legal custody determines the decision-making power regarding a child's upbringing. Physical custody refers to where the child primarily resides. Child support calculations, influenced by factors like income and parental responsibilities, also play a crucial role, determining financial obligations to support the child's well-being. It's advisable to seek the guidance of a legal professional to navigate this emotionally-charged area. The wellbeing of the child is paramount, and informed decision-making can mitigate potential long-term conflicts.

Spousal support, or alimony, presents yet another layer of complexity. The court considers several factors when determining its necessity, amount, and duration. Factors such as earning potential, the length of the marriage, and contributions of each spouse are carefully assessed. Modifications and terminations of spousal support orders are also possible under specific circumstances, requiring a thorough understanding of the legal provisions governing these changes. A well-informed approach, often involving legal counsel, is essential to ensure a just and equitable outcome.

Successfully navigating a divorce demands an understanding that extends beyond the simple dissolution of a marriage. The intricate legal processes involved, including asset division, child custody, and spousal support, often necessitate a comprehensive understanding of the relevant laws and procedures. It is vital to approach this process with informed preparation. This involves educating oneself about legal requirements or, ideally, securing competent legal representation. Remember that an equitable settlement isn't just about financial fairness; it's about achieving a resolution that supports the well-being of all those involved.

1.1 Grounds for Divorce

The most common ground for divorce varies considerably depending on the jurisdiction. In many places, "irreconcilable differences" is sufficient, essentially stating that the marriage has broken down irretrievably and there's no reasonable prospect of reconciliation. This is a broad category, encompassing a wide range of issues, from lack of communication to fundamental incompatibility of values and lifestyles. It's frequently chosen for its less adversarial nature compared to other grounds. However, remember this doesn't diminish the impact on those involved. Divorce, regardless of the legal basis, is emotionally and practically complex.

Some jurisdictions still adhere to more specific grounds, such as adultery, abandonment, or cruelty. Adultery, often requiring proof of a sexual relationship outside the marriage, can complicate proceedings and be highly emotionally charged. Abandonment, involving a spouse leaving the marital home without justification and the intent not to return, necessitates demonstration of both the physical separation and the intent. Proving cruel and inhumane treatment is challenging, and usually involves evidence of physical or emotional abuse; it requires a higher threshold of proof, meaning a clear and demonstrable pattern of harmful behaviour. This can be difficult to establish, requiring substantial evidence.

Legal separation is often a stepping stone or an alternative to divorce in some legal systems. This allows couples to live apart while maintaining certain legal ties, like property ownership or spousal support. It often addresses immediate financial and housing needs whilst delaying the finality of divorce. The process varies, and is sometimes treated like a temporary form of divorce, with separate stipulations and regulations. In some situations, legal separation might be used as a cooling-off period to try and reconcile, whereas in others it's a formal process leading to an eventual divorce. Consider the impact on finances; separate bank accounts may be required.

The specific requirements for proving grounds for divorce will depend entirely on the jurisdiction. Consult legal counsel in your state or province for specific details. It's crucial to obtain legal advice that is specific to your location; laws differ significantly. While "irreconcilable differences" offers a broader route, proving other grounds necessitates careful documentation and adherence to procedural rules. This can involve gathering evidence, such as emails, text messages, or witness testimonies. The legal process can feel overwhelming, but professional guidance is critical to navigate the specifics.

Choosing the appropriate ground for divorce often involves strategic considerations beyond simply establishing grounds. The choice can significantly affect the division of assets, child custody arrangements, and spousal support awards. Some grounds, especially those involving fault such as adultery or abuse, may influence the court's decisions in these matters. However, other jurisdictions prioritize equitable distribution of property regardless of fault. Understanding the potential consequences of different grounds necessitates a thorough consultation with a lawyer. The legal system can be complex; clear and specific advice is vital.

For instance, a claim of adultery might lead to a harsher outcome for the at-fault spouse in some jurisdictions, particularly regarding property division. However, in many jurisdictions, the emphasis is increasingly shifting away from assigning blame and towards equitable distribution regardless of fault. This means that the court's primary goal is to ensure a fair division of assets and responsibilities. Even if adultery or other grounds are cited, this does not guarantee a different outcome.

Gathering evidence to support claims, especially when involving allegations of adultery, abandonment or cruelty, needs careful consideration. It's advisable to maintain meticulous records, including dates, times, and corroborating evidence. Preserving any relevant communication, whether electronic or written, is crucial. The burden of proof rests on the individual filing for divorce; you must demonstrate the validity of your claim, usually according to a preponderance of the evidence. This means you need to show it's more likely than not that your claims are true.

Remember, the divorce process often involves emotional upheaval. Seeking support from friends, family, or therapists can greatly assist in coping with the stress involved. Even with legal representation, the emotional challenges can be immense. Maintaining a support system for emotional well-being is as critical as assembling the legal strategy. Take care of your mental health during this difficult time; self-care is essential. This is not just a legal battle; it's a significant life change.

1.2 Residency Requirements

Establishing residency before initiating divorce proceedings is crucial, and the specific requirements vary significantly by state. Understanding these requirements is paramount to ensuring your case is heard in the correct jurisdiction. Failure to meet these requirements could lead to delays, increased costs, or even dismissal of your petition. It's essential to familiarize yourself with your state's specific rules, which are usually outlined clearly in relevant legal statutes and case law. Consult legal resources or a qualified attorney for guidance.

Many states require a minimum period of residency within the state before you can file for divorce. This might range from six months to a year or even longer, depending on the state's laws. This continuous physical presence is typically demonstrable through documentation like utility bills, tax returns, or lease agreements proving consistent habitation in the state. Moreover, consider the concept of "domicile," often an additional requirement beyond mere residency. Domicile implies a more permanent intent to live in the state, implying a more than a temporary stay.

Beyond a minimum residency period, some jurisdictions may also impose additional requirements regarding your county or specific locality of residence. For instance, the state might mandate that you've resided within a particular county for a set length of time before filing, adding to the overall residency qualifications. Such specifications demonstrate that adhering to residency laws is not simply a matter of living within state lines but a more nuanced consideration of location and intentionality. Consequently, ignoring these subtleties can expose your case to potential legal challenges.

The complexities surrounding military personnel and their spouses further illustrate this point. Due to the nature of military service and frequent relocations, states often have specific provisions that address the residency requirements for individuals serving in the armed forces. These specialized rules may provide exceptions or different requirements, recognizing the unique circumstances and frequent moves associated with military life. The military status of one or both parties can thus heavily influence the jurisdiction where divorce proceedings are initiated.

Furthermore, the residency requirements don't solely concern the petitioner. In some cases, the laws stipulate the length of time your spouse must also reside in the state before the divorce can proceed. This dual-residency condition highlights the importance of examining not only your own residency status but also that of your spouse to determine the appropriate jurisdiction. Thus, the process often demands a careful assessment of both your situation and that of your partner in relation to jurisdictional laws.

Navigating residency requirements requires due diligence. Begin by consulting your state's statutes, which typically outline the exact residency period needed for divorce. These statutes are usually readily accessible online through your state's government website or legal databases. Additionally, consulting with a legal professional who specializes in family law is highly recommended. An attorney can ensure a thorough review of your specific circumstances and advise you on whether you meet the residency stipulations in your state. Seeking their help can help you avoid potential complications and delays.

Remember, these laws are constantly subject to change, so what might be true today could be obsolete tomorrow. Staying informed about any legal updates relevant to your state's divorce laws is crucial. This constant vigilance will ensure you comply with all current residency requirements and make sure your divorce proceeds smoothly and legally. It's also beneficial to check for any relevant case law, judicial interpretations of the statutes, which offer additional context for understanding their application in practice.

Ultimately, complying with residency requirements isn't simply a procedural formality; it's a cornerstone of a successful divorce case. It establishes the court's jurisdiction, ensuring that the case is rightfully heard in a relevant and competent court. Careful attention to detail and awareness of these specific rules minimizes the risk of costly delays or jeopardizing the legal standing of your divorce. Therefore, prioritize the thorough investigation and meticulous adherence to the established residency conditions of your state, always ensuring you meet all legal prerequisites.

Ignoring residency requirements carries significant risks, including but not limited to having your divorce petition dismissed. A dismissal would then require starting the entire process over again in a different jurisdiction, a process that may prove more time-consuming and expensive. Additionally, overlooking the details of residency requirements might lead to challenges from your spouse or their attorney, causing further delays and legal battles. Such complications emphasize the significance of diligently investigating and understanding these provisions before embarking on the divorce process.

Therefore, understanding and complying with residency requirements is not just advisable; it's legally necessary for the successful commencement and continuation of your divorce proceedings. Prioritize a thorough understanding of your state's specific laws, consult a family law expert for personalized guidance, and maintain awareness of any legal modifications that might impact your situation. This proactive approach will safeguard your rights and ensure a smoother, more efficient legal process in what can otherwise be a very difficult time in your life.

2 Chapter 2: Legal Representation

Finding the right lawyer is crucial. Don't just pick the first name you see in the phone book or the top result on a Google search. Take your time. Consider their experience in divorce cases, specifically those involving situations similar to yours. A lawyer specializing in high-net-worth divorces will have a different skill set than one handling simpler, less complex separations. Read online reviews, but understand that some may be biased. Talk to friends, family members, or even colleagues who have gone through a divorce. Their experience might offer valuable insights. Interview several lawyers before making a decision. This allows you to compare their communication styles, fees, and strategies. The best lawyer for you is one you trust, one who understands your situation, and one with whom you feel comfortable communicating openly and honestly. Choosing a lawyer is like choosing a partner in a battle; you need someone you can rely on.

Understanding the financial implications is paramount. Lawyer fees can vary widely depending on several factors. Some lawyers charge by the hour, others might take a contingency fee, a percentage of the settlement if they win your case, and still others might offer flat fees for specific services. Ask upfront about all costs involved – hourly rates, administrative fees, court costs, and expenses. Don't be afraid to negotiate. If their fees are beyond your budget, ask about payment plans. Open communication is key in this aspect. Many lawyers will work with you to ensure you can afford their services. Remember, a clear understanding of the costs beforehand prevents future surprises and potential financial strain during an already stressful time. Transparency is vital to building a strong attorney-client relationship based on trust and understanding. Inquire about any hidden costs or potential additional expenses. This is your right.

Attorney-client privilege is a cornerstone of the legal system, providing a crucial layer of protection. This privilege ensures that any communication between you and your lawyer remains confidential. This confidentiality extends to your personal details, your case strategy, and your private conversations. This is not a small matter. It shields your communications from unwanted disclosure, even from opposing counsel or the court, unless you explicitly waive that privilege. However, understand that it is not absolute. For instance, if you discuss committing a crime with your lawyer, this privilege is not protected. It safeguards your honest disclosures and allows you to freely discuss your case without worrying about damaging information being used against you. Use this shield; it's there to protect you. If you ever feel this privilege might be compromised, you need to immediately communicate with your lawyer.

Choosing a lawyer requires careful consideration. Don't rush the process. Gather information from various sources and carefully evaluate several candidates before making your decision. Remember that the relationship you build with your lawyer is crucial to the success of your case. Transparency and effective communication should be priorities in your selection process. This is an important decision and one that should not be taken lightly. Your lawyer will be your advocate, your guide, and your representative through a challenging process. The right choice can make all the difference in how the process unfolds and ultimately, in the outcome. Take the time to find someone you feel confident in, and someone who understands and respects your individual needs. Your financial well-being, future, and emotional state depend on this. This selection is about more than just legal expertise; it is about finding a trusted advisor who can help you navigate this challenging situation successfully.

Remember that your financial security depends on navigating the legal aspects of your divorce correctly. Seek clarity in all matters concerning fees, and never hesitate to ask questions. Your attorney's guidance is invaluable, and your proactive engagement is crucial to building a strong case and ensuring a positive outcome. A clear, open communication channel is essential for a successful legal strategy and a positive result. Protecting your privacy is paramount. Use the attorney-client privilege, but also remember its limits. The importance of open communication with your lawyer cannot be overstated, as it fosters trust and allows them to effectively represent your interests. Every step in the legal process is significant, so preparation, clarity, and informed decision-making are vital for achieving a fair and equitable outcome. Therefore, meticulous planning is crucial, and seeking professional legal counsel early is strongly recommended. Your ability to effectively navigate these complexities is crucial to your future.

2.1 Choosing a Lawyer

Finding the right lawyer is crucial; it's more than just picking a name from a directory. Your attorney will be your guide through a potentially turbulent and emotionally charged process, influencing the outcome significantly. Consider this chapter your roadmap to making a sound, informed decision.

Begin by identifying your specific needs. Are you primarily concerned with child custody arrangements? Is the division of property your biggest worry? Or are you facing complex financial issues requiring specialized expertise? Understanding your priorities will help you narrow your search. Don't hesitate to list them; prioritize what matters most.

Next, look for lawyers specializing in family law. General practitioners may handle divorces, but those with specific family law experience often possess deeper knowledge of relevant legislation, precedents, and strategies crucial for a successful outcome. This is not a time for generalists; accuracy is paramount and requires experience.

Check online reviews and ratings cautiously, keeping in mind that individual experiences vary considerably. Look for consistent themes rather than focusing solely on glowing praise or overly harsh criticism. Seek patterns and look for lawyers consistently praised for their communication, responsiveness, and legal acumen, rather than just their friendliness or quick resolution of cases.

Don't solely rely on online resources. Ask for referrals from trusted sources—friends, family members, or financial advisors—who've navigated similar situations. Personal recommendations provide valuable insight into a lawyer's character, competence, and work style. Networking is powerful; people often know experts beyond the reach of Google searches.

Schedule initial consultations with several lawyers before making a decision. These consultations often provide a limited free timeframe for you to ask questions; prepare a list in advance. Assess each lawyer's communication style, their ability to explain complex legal concepts clearly, and the overall feeling of trust and rapport that you develop. The best lawyer is someone you trust implicitly with your deepest concerns.

Pay close attention to the lawyer's fee structure. Understand how they bill their time, what services are included, and what additional expenses you might incur. Transparency regarding costs is essential, so you're fully informed about the financial implications of engaging their services; some lawyers work on contingency; understand their terms.

Remember, the initial consultation is as much about them getting to know you as it is about you evaluating them. Be open and honest about your case and expectations. A strong attorney-client relationship is built on mutual trust and understanding. This partnership will require open communication.

Finally, don't hesitate to seek a second opinion. If you're unsure about a particular lawyer's advice or approach, another consultation can provide a fresh perspective and potentially confirm your choice or encourage reconsideration. The legal process is not trivial; multiple opinions could be beneficial.

Choosing a lawyer is a significant decision, impacting the outcome of your divorce. By taking your time, asking the right questions, and following these steps, you can increase your chances of finding an attorney who will effectively represent your interests and guide you through this challenging period. The peace of mind that comes with having a skilled and trustworthy attorney by your side is invaluable. Don't rush this process; your future hinges on it.

2.2 Understanding Fees

Legal fees in divorce cases can be substantial, varying widely based on numerous factors. Understanding these factors is crucial for budgeting and managing expectations. The complexity of your case, for example, significantly impacts the overall cost. A straightforward, uncontested divorce with minimal assets will naturally cost less than a highly contested case involving significant property, business interests, or complex custody arrangements. Remember, time is money; protracted litigation leads to higher bills.

Your lawyer's hourly rate is a primary determinant of expense. Rates vary considerably depending on their experience, specialization (family law expertise is particularly crucial), and geographical location. Some lawyers may offer flat fees for specific services, such as preparing initial documents or representing you in mediation. However, be aware that these flat fees often pertain to simpler cases. Complex cases usually require an hourly rate structure. Contingency fees, where the lawyer's compensation is a percentage of the outcome, are generally not used in divorce cases. This is because the "outcome" is often a complex arrangement of property division, spousal support, and child custody, not a simple monetary award like in personal injury cases. While some lawyers might offer limited contingency arrangements for specific aspects, this is unusual and should be approached cautiously. It's vital to discuss the fee structure transparently with your lawyer from the outset, ensuring complete clarity about what services are included and how they will be billed. Don't hesitate to ask for a written fee agreement outlining all costs.

Beyond the lawyer's fees, you should also anticipate additional costs associated with your case. Court filing fees are a common expense, which vary by jurisdiction. Expert witness fees, such as those for appraisers (to value assets like real estate or businesses), accountants (to determine the value of financial accounts or businesses), or child custody evaluators, can add significantly to the total. Costs for document preparation, such as copying, scanning and sending documents, should also be considered. Additionally, you may need to pay for mediation services if you choose that route.

Effective communication with your lawyer is paramount to keeping costs manageable. Precisely outlining your goals, limiting unnecessary motions or requests for discovery and focusing on efficient strategies with your lawyer can prevent unnecessarily prolonged litigation. Openly discuss potential expenses and your budget constraints; your lawyer can then help you prioritize strategies and manage costs effectively. Consider whether you need representation for every aspect of the case; in some instances, you might represent yourself for less complex elements to reduce fees, with your attorney handling the more legally challenging aspects.

Remember, legal representation is an investment in your future. While cost is a valid concern, choosing the right lawyer based on experience and expertise should not be compromised simply to save money. A highly skilled lawyer with a thorough understanding of family law can often navigate complex situations more efficiently, sometimes minimizing overall costs in the long run, even though their hourly rate might be higher initially. Moreover, their expertise can ensure a more favorable outcome for you, potentially safeguarding your interests regarding assets, child custody, and support. Ultimately, careful planning and open communication with your attorney are key to understanding and managing the often considerable financial implications of a divorce. Proactive budgeting and a clear understanding of all possible expenses will contribute significantly towards a smoother and more financially controlled process.

2.3 Attorney-Client Privilege

The attorney-client privilege is a cornerstone of our legal system, particularly crucial during the emotionally charged process of divorce. It's a fundamental right, guaranteeing confidentiality between you and your lawyer. This confidentiality extends to all communications, whether written, verbal, or electronic. This means anything you discuss with your attorney, including personal details, financial information, and strategies, remains protected from disclosure. Think of it as a sacred space where you can openly and honestly share all aspects of your case without fear of that information being used against you. This protection fosters trust, enabling you to fully cooperate with your lawyer and receive the best possible legal advice. This freedom to communicate openly is essential for building a strong defense and achieving a fair resolution in your divorce.

However, understanding its scope is vital. While the privilege is extensive, it isn't absolute. Certain exceptions exist. For example, if you communicate with your attorney about future crimes or fraudulent activities, that information isn't protected. Similarly, if a court orders disclosure, your lawyer may be compelled to reveal privileged information, though this is rare and usually only happens under strict judicial oversight. The aim is to preserve the integrity of the legal process while protecting the client's fundamental right to privacy. Your lawyer should thoroughly explain these limitations to ensure you fully grasp the extent of the protection offered. Remember, any waivers you might sign must be clearly understood before signing them, and this should be done with the assistance of your attorney.

Maintaining this privilege requires conscious effort. Avoid discussing your case in informal settings, such as public places or social media, where conversations could be overheard. It's crucial to only communicate with your attorney and their designated staff through secure channels such as personal meetings, encrypted emails or secure messaging systems. Sending sensitive details via unencrypted email or leaving confidential documents in unsecured places risks waiving the privilege. Be diligent in protecting this vital right. Your lawyer will guide you on appropriate communication methods. Remember, the aim is always to maintain an exclusive line of communication exclusively between your legal representative and yourself. This will aid the process and will ensure a higher standard of work.

This privilege isn't just about keeping information secret; it's about encouraging frank and open communication. Your lawyer needs a complete and accurate picture of your circumstances to give you effective legal advice and represent you properly. With the privilege in place, you can share all the details — both positive and negative — without fear of judgment or reprisal. This allows your attorney to develop a robust legal strategy tailored to your unique situation. A lack of complete and full transparency would limit this process and will impact negatively your chances to secure a better outcome. Full transparency and an open communication path is always the best route.

Remember, this protection is invaluable in navigating the complexities of divorce. It enables you to strategize openly with your lawyer, explore various solutions, and ultimately, secure the best possible outcome. It's a shield against unwanted disclosure and a key element in your journey to a fair resolution. Understand the privilege's boundaries and actively safeguard it. It's a critical tool in your legal arsenal and an integral part of building a successful case. The significance of this privilege extends beyond the mere confidentiality of communications; it creates an environment where trust and cooperation between you and your attorney can fully flourish.

This confidentiality, however, doesn't extend to certain types of information. For instance, if you reveal to your attorney that you plan to commit a crime or have committed one in the past, that information is not privileged. Likewise, your attorney isn't obligated to maintain confidentiality if you're threatening to harm yourself or others. These exceptions are in place to protect public safety and uphold the law's integrity, while striking a balance between the client's need for privacy and the well-being of society. Transparency and honest communication remain key but must align with the law's ethics and principles.

The attorney-client privilege is not a mere formality; it's a cornerstone of legal representation and is a crucial part of ensuring a fair and just process. It's vital to actively preserve this privilege throughout your divorce proceedings. This is not only a legal right but also a foundational aspect of building a strong and trusting relationship with your attorney. Only with this foundation in place can you expect to receive the highest quality legal counsel, allowing you to navigate the complexities of your divorce with confidence and the support of a dedicated legal professional. This is one of the most important aspects of obtaining legal counsel during your divorce and must be fully understood and respected.

Understanding and safeguarding the attorney-client privilege is, therefore, paramount in the context of your divorce proceedings. Your lawyer's role extends beyond merely offering legal advice, they become a crucial confidant and advisor. This relationship is only possible within the confines of this privilege, providing you with a safe and secure space to share all the essential details of your case without fear of exposure or repercussions. A successful divorce proceeding will heavily rely on this aspect and should be prioritized above all.

Finally, remember that the attorney-client privilege is a powerful tool and a fundamental right. Utilize it fully, but always be aware of the limitations and exceptions. Consult with your attorney if you have any questions about the privilege or if you're unsure about the nature of a particular communication. Active engagement in understanding and protecting this right can significantly influence the outcome of your case, ensuring that your interests are fully protected and your privacy is respected throughout the process. Your peace of mind relies heavily on this, and taking steps to safeguard this privilege will aid in the process. Engage with your attorney and allow them to help you secure your rights.

3 Chapter 3: Asset Division

Determining what constitutes marital property is crucial. It's not simply everything acquired during the marriage; instead, it involves a careful assessment of each asset's origin and how it was acquired. Separate property, belonging solely to one spouse, remains untouched by the division process, unless it's been commingled with marital assets, obscuring the lines. For example, inherited jewelry remains the separate property of the inheriting spouse. However, if that jewelry was later used as collateral for a joint loan, its separate nature is jeopardized, complicating the division process and necessitating careful legal consideration.

Valuation of assets presents another significant hurdle. A house's worth requires a professional appraisal, ensuring an accurate assessment that stands up in court. Similarly, stocks, bonds, and businesses need thorough evaluation by experts who can understand their intricacies and provide a realistic valuation for equitable distribution. A poorly valued asset can lead to an unfair settlement, resulting in significant financial disadvantage for one party, making professional evaluation essential for fairness.

Equitable distribution, a cornerstone of most divorce proceedings, doesn't necessarily mean equal division. Instead, it aims for a fair distribution considering each spouse's contribution to the marriage, economic circumstances, and the overall fairness of the outcome. This requires a nuanced approach, accounting for factors like the length of the marriage, the earning potential of each spouse, and any significant disparities in contributions throughout the marriage. Disputes frequently arise regarding contributions, highlighting the importance of meticulous documentation. Debt division mirrors asset division; it is not a simple splitting of bills. Joint debts, such as mortgages and credit card balances, are often divided proportionally or according to each spouse's responsibility, while separate debts remain the sole responsibility of the individual who incurred them. However, the complexity arises when dealing with debts incurred during the marriage, particularly if one spouse's spending habits significantly contributed to the debt accumulation. Clearly defining the source of the debt and apportioning responsibility according to the relevant circumstances are crucial.

Retirement accounts often prove challenging. These accounts are frequently significant assets, representing years of contributions and accrued growth. Dividing these funds involves complex calculations and often mandates Qualified Domestic Relations Orders (QDROs) to ensure compliance with tax laws and the protection of each spouse's retirement security. Without a properly drafted QDRO, division of retirement assets can result in significant tax penalties or unexpected complications for one or both parties. Seeking expert guidance in this area prevents many potential problems.

Navigating the legal complexities of asset division is rarely straightforward. Even apparently simple cases can hide nuances and potential pitfalls. Inexperienced individuals often face difficulties in determining which assets are truly marital, how best to value them accurately, and in ensuring a truly equitable outcome. Thorough preparation, professional legal counsel, and a clear understanding of legal precedents are imperative to avoid costly and emotionally draining disputes. The process requires patience, a focus on practical solutions, and understanding the legal framework governing property distribution in divorce proceedings. Every divorce is unique. Your individual situation may require unique strategies and tailored solutions, which is why having the right legal guidance is absolutely essential. Failing to seek professional advice often leaves individuals vulnerable to financial and emotional exploitation, resulting in significantly less favorable outcomes. Therefore, securing qualified legal representation should not be seen as an added cost but rather a necessary investment in one's future. Remember to gather all relevant financial documentation, which includes bank statements, tax returns, and investment records. This enables a thorough understanding of your financial situation and assists your attorney in presenting a strong case. Moreover, being actively involved in the process, understanding the choices you make, and asking questions of your legal representative empowers you to navigate this challenging situation. The goal is not merely to survive the legal process but to emerge with a fair and just outcome.

3.1 Marital vs. Separate Property

The cornerstone of equitable property division in a divorce lies in clearly distinguishing between marital and separate property. Marital property, generally defined as assets acquired during the marriage, is subject to division between the spouses. This includes everything from the family home and vehicles to investment accounts and retirement funds accumulated during the union. The exact definition can vary slightly by state, however, so consulting with legal counsel in your specific jurisdiction is essential to ensure an accurate understanding of applicable laws. Ignoring this nuance could lead to significant financial repercussions.

Separate property, conversely, consists of assets owned by a spouse before the marriage, acquired during the marriage through inheritance or gift, or specifically designated as separate property through a prenuptial agreement. This is property that, under most circumstances, remains solely with the owning spouse during and after the dissolution of the marriage. It's vital to meticulously document all separate property, providing clear evidence of ownership predating the marriage or substantiating its acquisition through inheritance or gift. This documentation becomes crucial during the division of assets, protecting your interests from potential disputes.

Consider, for instance, a scenario where one spouse owned a business prior to the marriage. The business's value at the time of the marriage marks the baseline for assessing separate versus marital property. Any increase in the business's value during the marriage typically constitutes marital property and is subject to division, while the initial value remains separate property. Similarly, an inheritance received during the marriage remains separate property. However, the income generated from that inheritance during the marriage often becomes marital property.

Navigating these complexities requires careful attention to detail and often professional guidance. A common mistake is failing to accurately account for all assets, leading to unfair distribution. Accurate valuation of assets is critical. This requires professional appraisals for high-value items such as real estate, antiques, or artwork. Overlooking this step can lead to significantly undervaluing or overvaluing assets, negatively impacting the final settlement. The lack of proper valuation may cause one party to forfeit far more than they should, or vice-versa.

Furthermore, remember that debts are also subject to division. Joint debts incurred during the marriage are typically divided equitably. However, debts incurred solely by one spouse before the marriage or for personal reasons usually remain the responsibility of that spouse alone. This requires a comprehensive review of all financial obligations, including credit card debt, mortgages, and loans. Open and honest communication about debts is vital; hiding debts can severely compromise the fairness of the asset division and create lasting resentment between the parties, long after the divorce has been finalized.

Retirement accounts often represent a significant portion of a couple's assets, necessitating careful consideration during the division process. The division methods can vary depending on the type of plan (401(k), IRA, pension, etc.) and the governing laws. Qualified Domestic Relations Orders (QDROs) are frequently utilized to divide retirement assets, ensuring the proper transfer of funds without incurring tax penalties. Working with qualified financial and legal professionals is essential to navigate the intricacies of retirement asset division. A poorly executed division could mean a significant reduction in your retirement savings for years to come.

Ultimately, understanding the distinction between marital and separate property is paramount to a fair and equitable division of assets during a divorce. Accurate documentation, professional appraisals, and transparent communication are essential steps in protecting your interests throughout the process. Proactive measures in gathering information and preparing for the asset division process far before the divorce proceedings begin are always advisable. Remember that this process is often emotionally charged, and legal guidance ensures a more objective and equitable outcome. The emotional impact can often cloud judgment, so seeking advice from qualified professionals becomes even more crucial.

3.2 Valuation of Assets

Accurately valuing assets during a divorce is paramount for a fair and equitable settlement. This process often involves professional appraisals, meticulous documentation, and a thorough understanding of various asset types. Failing to accurately assess the value of assets can lead to significant financial disadvantages for one or both parties, potentially resulting in protracted legal battles and increased legal costs. It's crucial to remember that even seemingly simple assets require careful consideration.

Determining the value of real estate, for instance, isn't as straightforward as looking at recent comparable sales. While these offer a starting point, a professional appraisal accounts for many nuanced factors affecting property value including but not limited to location, condition, market fluctuations, and any unique features. This is especially important if the property is a primary residence with substantial sentimental value, or if it has unique features, such as an extensive garden or waterfront access, impacting its marketability. The appraisal must account for these specifics to avoid undervaluing or overvaluing the asset.

Businesses present an even more complex valuation challenge. A simple balance sheet snapshot is insufficient; a thorough review of financial statements, projected income streams, and intangible assets such as brand recognition or intellectual property is essential. Professional business valuation services are often necessary, especially for larger or more complex ventures. These specialized services provide an unbiased, professionally detailed assessment of a business's market worth, a critical step in ensuring a fair division of assets. This assessment should consider not only current market conditions but also future prospects, taking into account things like existing contracts, market trends and competitive landscapes.

Retirement accounts, often a significant marital asset, require careful handling. These accounts, including 401(k)s, IRAs, and pensions, represent future income streams and need to be evaluated based on their projected future value, which can be a complex calculation using actuarial tables and considering the spouse's age and expected lifespan. Dividing these assets frequently involves Qualified Domestic Relations Orders (QDROs) which are complex legal documents that must be carefully drafted by an attorney to ensure compliance with both tax laws and divorce decree requirements. Errors in this process can lead to significant tax penalties.

Personal property, ranging from jewelry and artwork to vehicles and collectibles, requires a systematic approach to valuation. Insurance appraisals or recent purchase receipts can be helpful starting points. However, for unique or valuable items, a professional appraisal might be necessary to determine market value, taking into account factors like age, condition, rarity, and authenticity. It's important to meticulously document everything, creating a comprehensive inventory with supporting documentation for each item. Photographs and detailed descriptions prove cru-

cial for evidentiary purposes, should disputes arise.
Bank accounts and other financial assets, while seemingly straightforward, still require careful attention. The balance on the date of separation serves as the initial value, although any interest accrued subsequently may be divided based on the court's stipulations. Furthermore, the identification and valuation of assets held in trusts, investment accounts, or other complex financial vehicles necessitates the help of financial professionals to provide an accurate assessment and to explain those details to the court. They may have their own methods for calculating their value. It's crucial to accurately reflect the values within the court documents.
In summary, accurately valuing assets during a divorce is a multifaceted process demanding a thorough and detailed approach. This involves careful attention to the specifics of each asset category, often necessitating the expertise of professional appraisers and financial advisors to ensure an equitable outcome. Thorough documentation and meticulous record-keeping are essential to support valuations and prevent disputes. Remember, seeking professional advice is critical; this chapter provides a general overview, but individual circumstances require tailored solutions. Ignoring these complexities can have costly consequences, potentially undermining the fairness of the entire divorce process. A well-documented and expertly assessed valuation lays the groundwork for a more amicable and just settlement.

3.3 Equitable Distribution

Fairness is the cornerstone of equitable distribution in divorce proceedings. It's not about splitting everything down the middle; it's about achieving a just and reasonable division of assets and debts accumulated during the marriage. This requires careful consideration of numerous factors, and a thorough understanding of the legal principles involved. Ignoring these aspects can lead to significant financial disadvantages, prolonging the already emotionally challenging process.

Understanding the concept of marital property is crucial. This encompasses all assets acquired during the marriage, regardless of who technically holds the title. This can range from tangible assets like real estate and vehicles to intangible assets such as retirement accounts, stocks, and business interests. Conversely, separate property consists of assets owned prior to the marriage or received during the marriage as gifts or inheritances. Clearly distinguishing between these two categories is paramount for a fair division.

The valuation of assets is equally important. This isn't simply about listing the current market price. For complex assets, such as a family business or unique artwork, professional appraisal may be needed to provide accurate and objective valuations. This ensures both parties receive a fair share based on the true worth of the assets, minimizing disputes and potential legal battles. Accurate valuation prevents one party from being unfairly disadvantaged by a skewed assessment.

Determining what constitutes "equitable" distribution isn't always straightforward. While the goal is fairness, the exact method varies by jurisdiction. Some states mandate equal division of marital property, while others consider factors like contributions of each spouse, duration of the marriage, and the economic circumstances of each party. Understanding your specific state's laws is critical to navigating this phase of the divorce process successfully, avoiding unnecessary complications.

The division of debt is just as significant as the division of assets. Marital debts, those incurred during the marriage, are generally divided in the same manner as assets. This includes credit card debt, mortgages, and loans. Separate debts, those accumulated before the marriage or received as a result of individual actions, usually remain the responsibility of the individual who incurred them. However, it's essential to ensure that debt allocation is clearly defined and documented to prevent future disputes and financial hardship.

Retirement accounts present unique challenges in equitable distribution. These accounts, often representing a substantial portion of a couple's net worth, require specialized handling. Qualified Domestic Relations Orders (QDROs) are frequently used to divide retirement assets fairly. A QDRO is a court order specifying how a retirement plan will be divided between the divorcing spouses, ensuring that funds are transferred legally and tax-efficiently. Obtaining expert legal and financial advice is critical to manage this complex process effectively.

Beyond the specific assets and debts, the overall financial picture of each spouse must be considered. Factors such as earning potential, future expenses, and existing financial obligations play a significant role in determining an equitable outcome. Judges often consider the long-term financial stability of each party, striving to avoid leaving one spouse at a significant financial disadvantage. This comprehensive approach aims to ensure a fair and sustainable settlement for both parties.

Navigating the complexities of equitable distribution requires meticulous preparation and often, professional assistance. Gathering all relevant financial documents, including bank statements, tax returns, and investment records, is paramount. Organizing this information in a clear and accessible manner will facilitate a smoother and more efficient process, enhancing the effectiveness of negotiations and ultimately, contributing to the overall fairness of the outcome.

Remember, equitable distribution aims to create a fair and just settlement, but it's not a zero-sum game. While it's vital to advocate for your rights and interests, constructive collaboration and open communication can significantly enhance the chances of achieving a mutually agreeable outcome. Mediation, often assisted by skilled professionals, can be a valuable tool in facilitating discussions and finding common ground. Working towards a cooperative solution, even in the face of conflict, can reduce stress, expense, and ultimately create a more positive transition for all involved.

Finally, remember that legal guidance is invaluable throughout this process. An experienced family law attorney can help you understand the laws in your jurisdiction, navigate the complexities of asset valuation, negotiate effectively, and protect your rights. Seeking professional advice will ensure your interests are protected, allowing you to focus on the emotional aspects of the divorce while maintaining control of your future financial security. Don't underestimate the value of skilled legal counsel in this process; it can significantly impact the fairness and longevity of your settlement.

3.4 Division of Debt

Debt, a frequent unwelcome guest in even the happiest marriages, transforms into a particularly thorny issue during divorce. The division of debt isn't simply about splitting bills down the middle; it's about meticulously untangling financial obligations, understanding individual responsibilities, and ensuring a fair and legally sound outcome. This process often requires careful documentation and, frequently, professional legal guidance.

Understanding the difference between joint and separate debt is crucial. Joint debts, those incurred during the marriage, are generally considered marital debt and subject to division. Separate debts, those predating the marriage or acquired individually during the marriage (like a personal loan), usually remain the responsibility of the individual who incurred them. However, complexities arise, especially when commingling of funds blurs the lines between separate and joint accounts. For example, if separate funds were used to pay down a joint debt, careful accounting becomes necessary to determine the fair share each party owes.

The process often begins with a thorough inventory of all debts. This includes credit card balances, mortgages, student loans, personal loans, and any other financial obligations. Each debt should be meticulously documented, including the creditor's name, the account number, the outstanding balance, and the monthly payment. Obtaining credit reports for both spouses provides a comprehensive overview of their individual and joint financial standing. Discrepancies or disputes necessitate further investigation, perhaps involving the assistance of a financial advisor or forensic accountant.

Determining the equitable distribution of debt is frequently the most challenging aspect. Courts typically consider the factors contributing to the accumulation of debt, each spouse's income and earning potential, and the needs of any dependent children. Simply dividing the total debt equally isn't always just; consideration must be given to who benefitted from the debt and the current financial capacity of each spouse to meet their obligations. For instance, a significant amount of debt incurred for one spouse's education could disproportionately impact their future earning potential, necessitating a different approach to debt allocation.

Legal agreements or court orders solidify the division of debt. The specifics of these agreements will vary depending on jurisdiction and the specific circumstances of each case. They may entail one spouse assuming responsibility for specific debts, while the other receives a corresponding share of assets. Alternatively, both parties may share the burden of particular debts, with adjustments made to alimony or child support payments. Regardless of the approach, a written and legally binding agreement is essential to avoid future disputes and ensure clarity regarding individual responsibilities.

Negotiation and compromise play a pivotal role in resolving debt division disputes. Open and honest communication between spouses, facilitated perhaps by a mediator or attorney, can help reach an agreement that satisfies both parties' needs and aligns with their individual financial capabilities. This collaborative approach minimizes acrimony and reduces the financial and emotional costs often associated with lengthy legal battles. While this may necessitate relinquishing some desired outcomes, it ultimately fosters a more constructive resolution, paving the way for a smoother post-divorce transition.

Remember, seeking professional legal advice is crucial. Attorneys specializing in family law possess in-depth knowledge of relevant laws and regulations governing debt division, ensuring your rights are protected and the process proceeds fairly. They can guide you through the complexities of financial documentation, negotiation strategies, and legal processes, offering invaluable support during a challenging time. Do not underestimate the importance of this expertise, as the financial ramifications of an improperly handled debt division can be significant and long-lasting.

Failure to address debt division adequately can lead to ongoing financial stress and disputes long after the divorce is finalized. Careful planning, meticulous documentation, and an understanding of legal rights and responsibilities are essential to securing a financially stable future for both parties. Navigating the division of debt requires patience, persistence, and a commitment to seeking professional support when needed. This investment of time and resources will ultimately result in a more equitable and long-term sustainable outcome. The ultimate goal is a clear, legally sound resolution, allowing both parties to move forward with their financial lives in a more stable and secure manner. Remember, effective communication and professional guidance are your most valuable allies in this process. Don't hesitate to seek support; your future financial well-being depends on it.

3.5 Retirement Accounts

Retirement accounts often represent a significant portion of a couple's accumulated wealth, making their division during divorce particularly complex. These accounts, including 401(k)s, IRAs, and pensions, often involve intricate calculations and potential tax implications that require careful consideration. Understanding the different types of retirement plans and their implications for divorce is crucial for a fair and equitable settlement. Failing to address these accounts appropriately can lead to long-term financial hardship for one or both parties.

The process begins with accurate valuation. Determining the current market value of each retirement account is paramount. This requires obtaining official statements from the plan administrators detailing the account balance as of a specific date. In cases of highly volatile investments, multiple valuations may be necessary to ensure fairness. Furthermore, the value of any future employer contributions must be considered, especially when these contributions are expected to significantly increase the account's total value over time. Accurate valuation forms the basis for a just division of these valuable assets.

Many states employ the concept of "equitable distribution" when dividing marital assets, including retirement accounts. This means that assets are divided fairly, but not necessarily equally. The court will consider factors such as the length of the marriage, each spouse's contribution to the accumulation of the assets, and the earning capacity of each party. In some cases, a judge may order a "qualified domestic relations order," or QDRO, to specify how the retirement assets will be divided. This legal document is essential for the proper transfer of funds and ensures compliance with federal and state regulations governing retirement plan distributions. It's crucial to understand that a QDRO is a complex legal document and should only be prepared by a qualified attorney.

A QDRO allows for a portion of the retirement account to be transferred directly to the non-employee spouse's own retirement account without triggering immediate tax consequences. This protects the assets from premature taxation and allows for the continued growth of the retirement savings. However, the process of obtaining a QDRO can be protracted, involving negotiations be-

tween parties and the plan administrator. It also requires meticulous attention to detail to ensure the order accurately reflects the court's decision. An experienced attorney can help navigate this complicated process, minimizing delays and ensuring accurate execution.
Another crucial aspect involves the tax implications of dividing retirement accounts. Distributions from retirement accounts before retirement age are generally subject to income tax and may also incur penalties. A QDRO, while avoiding immediate taxation, doesn't eliminate future tax liabilities upon distribution. Understanding these potential tax liabilities is crucial for both spouses to accurately assess their long-term financial implications and make informed decisions about the division. Professional tax advice is highly recommended to navigate these complexities and make financially sound choices.
The division of retirement assets can be far more intricate than the division of other marital property. Unlike readily divisible assets, retirement accounts involve complex legal and financial considerations. Navigating these complexities requires a clear understanding of the applicable laws, the valuation process, and the tax implications. Seeking professional help from experienced legal and financial advisors is highly recommended to ensure a fair and equitable settlement that protects your financial future. Failing to seek such assistance can have significant financial ramifications lasting far beyond the divorce process itself. The importance of accurate documentation, clear legal advice, and thorough understanding of the process cannot be overstated. The financial well-being of both parties often hinges on the successful and equitable division of retirement assets. This necessitates a cautious and carefully managed approach, guided by professionals adept

in this specialized area of family law. The intricacies of QDROs, tax implications, and the process of asset valuation demand expertise. So, protect your financial future. Don't navigate this alone.

4 Chapter 4: Child Custody

The most emotionally charged aspect of divorce, especially for those with children, often revolves around custody arrangements. Understanding the legal framework surrounding child custody is paramount, mitigating potential conflict and ensuring the child's best interests remain the priority. This involves grasping the fundamental differences between legal and physical custody, terms often misunderstood and misused, leading to unnecessary disputes. Legal custody refers to the parent's right to make major decisions concerning the child's upbringing – education, healthcare, religion. Physical custody, conversely, dictates the child's living arrangements and daily schedule. Sole custody grants one parent both legal and physical control, while joint custody shares these responsibilities between parents, potentially in a variety of ways, requiring clear, legally documented agreements.

Many jurisdictions prioritize the child's best interests as the ultimate determinant in custody decisions. This broad concept encompasses various factors considered by judges, such as the child's wishes (if they are of a certain age and maturity), the stability of each parent's home environment, the parental relationship, and each parent's ability to provide for the child's physical and emotional needs. These assessments are rarely straightforward, often necessitating psychological evaluations or social worker reports to furnish a comprehensive picture for the court. The process can feel invasive and emotionally draining, requiring patience and a clear focus on the child's well-being above all else. Remember to meticulously document everything, from your child's academic achievements to any instances of parental conflict, to present the most robust and convincing case possible.

Child support, intrinsically linked to custody, represents the financial obligation of one parent towards the child's upbringing. Calculating child support varies significantly across jurisdictions, with formulas often considering factors such as each parent's income, the number of children, and the custody arrangement. Understanding the specific formula and calculation used in your state is vital, allowing you to anticipate potential support obligations and negotiate effectively. While frustrating and complex, carefully reviewing and understanding these calculations is crucial in ensuring a fair and sustainable support agreement is reached. Seek advice from your attorney regarding your specific circumstances and local laws. They can analyze your case and aid in negotiating a favorable arrangement.

Negotiating child custody arrangements can be emotionally challenging, even more so when dealing with acrimonious divorce proceedings. Open communication, though difficult, remains essential. Attempting to maintain respectful dialogue with your former spouse, focusing on the child's needs above personal grievances, can significantly facilitate the process. Mediation, a structured process involving a neutral third party, often proves helpful in navigating disagreements and fostering compromise. Mediation can significantly reduce the time, stress, and expense of lengthy court battles, helping both parties arrive at a more equitable and amicable resolution. Remember the process is about your child; let that be your guiding principle.

While mediation often provides a more amicable and efficient resolution, litigation might become unavoidable. In such situations, building a strong legal case becomes imperative. This necessitates meticulous record-keeping, securing credible evidence, and diligently preparing for potential court appearances. Your attorney's expertise in family law is crucial, guiding you through the legal procedures and representing your best interests in court. Preparing yourself mentally for the possibility of court proceedings, understanding the potential emotional toll and the need for strong self-advocacy, is crucial for enduring a potentially lengthy and complex legal process. Remember to take care of yourself, both physically and emotionally, while navigating this difficult phase.

Despite the legal complexity, remembering the child's needs is paramount. The ideal outcome isn't simply a legally sound arrangement; it's one that promotes your child's well-being, offering stability, love, and the chance to thrive. Focusing on practical aspects like routines, co-parenting strategies, and ensuring consistent communication between parents – despite any personal difficulties – is key to creating a positive environment for your child. Seeking professional guidance, such as family counseling, can significantly aid in establishing healthy co-parenting dynamics, providing strategies for conflict resolution, and ensuring the child's emotional health remains a priority during the transition and beyond. Never underestimate the profound impact that a stable and loving environment has on a child's development. Your commitment to a healthy and cooperative co-parenting relationship will make all the difference to your child's well-being.

4.1 Legal vs. Physical Custody

Legal custody concerns a parent's right to make major decisions regarding their child's upbringing, such as education, healthcare, and religious affiliation. It's not about where the child sleeps or spends most of their time; instead, it grants one or both parents the authority to act as the child's legal guardian in significant matters. Think of it as the power to make the big calls. Joint legal custody, often favored by courts, allows both parents equal say, fostering collaboration and shared responsibility. However, sole legal custody grants decision-making power to a single parent, usually due to concerns about the other parent's suitability or capacity. This decision is not taken lightly and requires careful consideration of the child's best interests, often involving evidence presented to the court. A judge's ultimate decision rests on a comprehensive assessment of each parent's capabilities and the potential impact on the child's well-being.

Physical custody, conversely, determines the child's physical residence and living arrangements. It dictates where the child sleeps, eats, and spends their time. This element is often intricately linked to the child's daily routine and stability. Joint physical custody involves the child residing with both parents, often in alternating schedules, perhaps week-on, week-off, or a similar arrangement designed to maximize time spent with each parent. Such schedules require careful planning and communication to minimize disruption to the child's routine and well-being. Sole physical custody, however, means the child primarily resides with one parent, with the other parent typically having visitation rights. This arrangement is often implemented when concerns exist about one parent's suitability for providing a safe and stable home environment. The determination of physical custody involves careful evaluation of factors like the child's needs, the parents' living situations, and the potential impact on the child's emotional and psychological development. Ultimately, the goal is to establish a living situation that prioritizes the child's best interests above all else.

The interplay between legal and physical custody can be complex. It's entirely possible to have joint legal custody and sole physical custody, or vice versa. Imagine a scenario where parents share decision-making power (joint legal custody), but the child resides primarily with one parent (sole physical custody) due to logistical factors or parental preference. Conversely, a family might opt for sole legal custody with one parent making all significant decisions, while maintaining a robust schedule of joint physical custody, ensuring substantial time with both parents. Understanding the distinction is crucial; it's not always a simple equation of one equaling the other. The choices are multifaceted and deeply impact the child's life.

Navigating these arrangements requires clear communication and collaboration. Ideally, parents should strive for a solution that puts the child's well-being first. This often entails open dialogue, compromise, and potentially professional guidance, such as mediation or counseling. Agreements reached outside of court are often preferred, as they foster a sense of cooperation and avoid the adversarial nature of litigation. A collaborative approach can significantly reduce conflict and facilitate a smoother transition for both the parents and the child.

However, when parents cannot agree, court intervention becomes necessary. Judges weigh various factors when determining custody arrangements. These can include each parent's stability, their ability to provide a nurturing environment, the child's preferences (depending on their age and maturity), and any evidence of domestic violence or substance abuse. Court decisions are usually made in the best interests of the child, aiming to ensure their safety, well-being, and development. The legal process, though sometimes arduous, provides a framework for resolving disputes and establishing clear legal guidelines for parental responsibilities.

It's critical to remember that custody arrangements are not set in stone. Circumstances can change, requiring modifications to existing orders. For example, a change in employment, a move to a different location, or a significant shift in a parent's behavior could necessitate adjustments. These modifications often necessitate returning to court, presenting updated information and supporting evidence to justify the proposed changes. The court retains the power to review and alter custody arrangements if deemed necessary in the child's best interest.

Finally, seeking legal counsel is highly recommended during this process. An experienced family law attorney can provide invaluable guidance in navigating the intricacies of custody arrangements, negotiating with your ex-partner, preparing for court proceedings, and ensuring your rights are protected. Their expertise ensures you understand your options, choose the most appropriate course of action, and make informed decisions about your child's future. They're not just lawyers; they are advocates for you and your child during what can be a highly emotional and challenging time. Their role is to guide you through the legal labyrinth and support you in reaching a resolution that serves the child's best interests.

4.2 Child Support Calculations

Child support calculations are determined by various factors, most significantly the non-custodial parent's income and the number of children involved. State guidelines often provide a formula, incorporating these elements and sometimes accounting for extraordinary medical expenses or childcare costs. Understanding these calculations is crucial for both parents. Navigating this process without legal guidance can be extremely difficult, potentially leading to unfair or unequal outcomes. Therefore, seeking legal counsel is advisable to ensure your rights and your child's needs are adequately protected.

The specific formula used varies considerably by state. Some states utilize a percentage of the non-custodial parent's net income, while others use more complex formulas involving both parents' income and expenses. These differences highlight the importance of familiarizing yourself with your specific state's guidelines and legislation. Inconsistent applications of the law across jurisdictions underscore the need for local expertise. You should also expect variations based on factors like the child's age, educational needs, and any special needs or medical requirements.

Furthermore, deviations from the standard guidelines can occur. Judges possess discretion in certain situations, allowing adjustments based on individual circumstances. These circumstances could include the custodial parent's income, the child's extraordinary needs, or unusual family dynamics. For instance, a child requiring extensive medical care might necessitate a higher child support amount than standard formulas would calculate. Similarly, if one parent has significantly higher income than the other, the court may deviate from the strict formula to accommodate these substantial differences.

Beyond the monetary aspects, understanding the legal implications of child support is vital. Failure to comply with court-ordered payments can lead to serious consequences, including wage garnishment, license suspension, and even contempt of court charges. These consequences can severely impact your financial stability and credit rating. Promptly addressing any concerns regarding payment or modifications to child support orders is essential to avoiding such penalties. Remember, open communication with your legal counsel regarding your financial status and any potential changes in your circumstances will help in preventing severe consequences.

Successfully navigating child support calculations frequently requires a balance of legal understanding and financial transparency. Maintain detailed financial records, including pay stubs, tax returns, and bank statements. These records will prove invaluable during any child support calculation and subsequent review. Thorough documentation minimizes disputes and aids in establishing a clear financial picture for both parties and the court. The better prepared you are, the smoother and faster the whole legal process will be, ensuring you can focus on the best interests of your child. Proactive record-keeping is critical in this respect.

Finally, remember that child support calculations aren't static. Significant life changes, such as a change in employment, a substantial increase or decrease in income, or a change in the child's needs, might warrant a modification of the existing child support order. The courts have mechanisms for handling such adjustments. Proactively seeking a modification when such changes occur ensures continued fairness and adherence to the best interests of the child. Failing to do so could result in an outdated and potentially unfair child support arrangement. Thus, remaining vigilant and keeping your lawyer informed about any significant alterations in your financial or family situation is paramount in ensuring fairness and the best interests of your child.

5 Chapter 5: Spousal Support

Spousal support, often called alimony, is a complex area of divorce law. It involves one spouse providing financial assistance to the other after separation, a decision based on a variety of factors, not solely the length of the marriage. Judges consider each case individually, focusing on the relative economic circumstances and earning potential of both spouses. This differs from child support, which is specifically for the well-being of children.

The most significant factor influencing spousal support is the financial disparity between the two parties. A lengthy marriage often supports a longer period of support, particularly if one spouse significantly sacrificed career opportunities for the family's benefit. The length of the marriage itself does not automatically dictate the amount or duration, it's a piece of a larger puzzle. This sacrifice can be anything from forgoing a higher-paying job to taking on the primary caregiving role. Judges frequently use this information to determine the need for, and appropriateness of, spousal support.

Beyond financial disparity and length of the marriage, the judge also looks at the standard of living established during the marriage. Maintaining that standard of living for the financially dependent spouse, at least for a transition period, is often a priority. This is particularly relevant if one spouse has been a homemaker and lacks the marketable skills and work experience to rapidly obtain employment with similar compensation. Supporting that transition to independence is a common aim of spousal support. The recipient's ability to become self-supporting is a key consideration, influencing whether support is temporary or permanent, short term or long term.

Factors such as the age, health, and employability of each spouse also significantly impact the decision. A spouse with health issues that limit their work capacity may require extended support. Similarly, an older spouse with fewer years remaining in their career may receive more support than a younger, more readily employable individual. These considerations demonstrate that spousal support is not simply about punishing one party but ensuring a fair and equitable outcome given the unique circumstances of each divorce. The ability to pay, on the side of the supporting spouse, also enters the equation; an exorbitant amount of support that creates significant hardship would be unreasonable.

Modification or termination of spousal support is possible under specific circumstances. Significant changes in the financial status of either party can justify a review. For example, a substantial increase in the recipient's income or a decrease in the payer's income could lead to adjustments. Also, if the receiving spouse remarries, that often results in a termination of support, because that demonstrates a significant shift in their financial circumstances. This is not always automatic and still requires a court's review, where the reasons for the remarriage may affect the ruling. Similarly, the death of either party automatically terminates

spousal support.
The process of modifying or terminating spousal support typically involves filing a motion with the court, presenting evidence to support the request for modification or termination. This process can involve additional legal fees and court appearances, emphasizing the importance of clearly understanding and documenting any change in circumstances. Seeking legal counsel in these situations is highly recommended, as navigating these processes without professional help can be complicated and potentially detrimental to one's legal standing. Precise documentation is always advised.
Finally, remember that spousal support decisions are individualized. There's no universal formula. Each case rests on the unique blend of factors discussed. While these factors provide a framework, the ultimate decision rests with the judge, who must weigh all evidence and ensure an equitable outcome given the unique circumstances of the specific case. The process is designed to facilitate a fair transition, not punish one party, even when there is a dramatic power imbalance evident before the process. Therefore, understanding the numerous variables is key to navigating this critical aspect of divorce proceedings effectively. Seeking legal advice early on is crucial for developing a sound strategy and protecting your interests throughout the process. Open communication with your attorney can reduce the impact of this aspect of your divorce.

5.1 Factors Determining Support

The length of the marriage significantly influences spousal support awards. Longer marriages often result in longer support periods, reflecting the greater interdependence developed over time. Conversely, shorter marriages may lead to shorter or no support, as the economic interdependence might be less significant. Judges consider the duration as a key factor in determining the fairness and equity of the support arrangement. This element directly affects the amount of financial assistance provided and the timeframe for its provision.

Economic disparity between spouses is another crucial consideration. If one spouse earned significantly more during the marriage and contributed substantially to the family's financial well-being, the court might award support to the other spouse to ensure a reasonable standard of living post-separation. This often involves an assessment of earning capacity, employment history, and the potential for future income. The goal is to prevent one spouse from experiencing a drastic decline in their lifestyle while the other enjoys a continued affluent position. The greater the difference, the stronger the argument for support.

The spouse's ability to be self-supporting plays a pivotal role. Courts assess the recipient spouse's potential to become financially independent. This evaluation includes factors like employment history, skills, education, and health. If a spouse demonstrates a strong capacity for self-sufficiency, the court may reduce or eliminate support. Conversely, if a spouse lacks the skills or health to secure gainful employment, the need for support increases. The assessment isn't solely about current employment but also about the realistic potential for future earning capacity.

The health and mental condition of each spouse is also relevant. A spouse's physical or mental health challenges can significantly impact their ability to work and maintain self-sufficiency. Preexisting conditions, illnesses, or injuries incurred during the marriage may be considered. This requires a comprehensive assessment of medical records and expert testimony if necessary. The severity and impact of such conditions directly affect the likelihood and amount of support awarded, ensuring a fair consideration of limitations imposed by health circumstances.

The standard of living established during the marriage is critical. Courts strive to maintain a reasonable standard of living for both spouses, particularly for the recipient. This requires an examination of the couple's lifestyle during the marriage—their expenses, assets, and overall quality of life. The objective is to prevent a significant decline in the recipient's lifestyle, although it does not necessarily guarantee maintaining the exact same standard. A court aims to balance fairness with financial reality, avoiding unreasonable burdens on either party.

The contributions of each spouse to the marriage, both financial and non-financial, matter significantly. While financial contributions are easily quantifiable, non-financial contributions such as childcare, homemaking, or supporting a spouse's career are harder to assess. However, these contributions are not disregarded. Evidence of such contributions can bolster a claim for spousal support, recognizing the substantial value of these often-uncompensated roles. Judges carefully weigh all contributions to achieve equitable outcomes.

The presence of children and their needs significantly influence spousal support decisions. The caregiving responsibilities associated with raising children often affect a spouse's ability to work and earn income. The age and needs of the children further impact this, as young children require more intensive care. The court must consider the financial burden of childcare and the potential impact on the supporting spouse's earning capacity. This dynamic

significantly influences support awards.
The conduct of the parties, particularly instances of abuse or abandonment, can affect support orders. If one spouse engages in behavior that significantly harms the other, it can influence the court's decision. This includes domestic violence, adultery, or desertion. These actions are not determinative factors but can be relevant when assessing the overall fairness and equity of the support award. The court aims to ensure a just outcome, acknowledging any detrimental actions within the marriage.
Finally, the length of the support order itself is carefully considered. It isn't an open-ended commitment. The court assesses the length of support based on various factors discussed earlier: the length of the marriage, the spouse's ability to become self-supporting, and the children's needs. The duration is designed to provide temporary assistance to achieve self-sufficiency, not indefinite reliance. Support agreements often include provisions for modification or termination under specific circumstances. The goal is to help the supported spouse regain financial independence within a reasonable timeframe.

5.2 Modification of Support

Circumstances change. That's a fundamental truth, and it's especially relevant in the aftermath of a divorce. Spousal support orders, carefully crafted during the initial proceedings, may become outdated or inequitable as time marches on. This chapter focuses on the modification of spousal support, a process requiring careful navigation of legal intricacies and a clear understanding of your rights. It is not a simple task, but with the right knowledge, it's achievable.

Successfully modifying a support order necessitates a compelling reason for the change. Simply feeling dissatisfied isn't enough. Courts require evidence of a substantial and material change in circumstances, something beyond the normal ups and downs of life. This could encompass a significant job loss resulting in a dramatic reduction in income, a serious illness requiring extensive medical expenses, or a substantial increase in the recipient's income, demonstrating self-sufficiency. Document everything meticulously. Keep records of income statements, medical bills, and any other documentation that substantiates your claim.

The process itself often starts with filing a formal motion with the court. This motion should clearly state the reasons for the requested modification, providing detailed evidence supporting your claim. Be prepared to present this evidence in court. Your attorney will guide you through this process. Don't try to navigate this alone; this process is highly complex and demands professional legal assistance.

Remember, the court will review the original support order, considering the factors that initially determined its terms. They'll then assess whether the newly presented circumstances warrant a modification. This analysis can involve scrutinizing income levels, expenses, health conditions, and the needs of each party. The process might involve discovery, where both parties exchange financial information and relevant documents. Full cooperation is vital, though your lawyer will always advocate for your best interests.

Financial transparency is crucial. The court expects accurate and complete financial disclosure from both parties. Failure to disclose assets or income could jeopardize your case and potentially lead to negative consequences. Remember, honesty is not merely the best policy; it's often a legal requirement. Any attempt at concealment will likely hurt you in the long run.

Each state has its own specific rules and regulations concerning the modification of spousal support orders. The legal standards may vary significantly, affecting the ease or difficulty of your modification application. Your lawyer is familiar with these rules and will ensure your action aligns with your jurisdiction's guidelines, avoiding unnecessary delays or complications. Understanding these variations beforehand is paramount for success.

Beyond financial factors, the court will assess whether the change impacts the recipient's ability to maintain their standard of living. If the modification leaves the recipient in a position of significant hardship, the court may be less inclined to grant the requested change. Therefore, careful consideration of the recipient's circumstances is critical to your strategy. Your attorney will help you navigate this delicate aspect.

The duration of the modification process is unpredictable. It can vary significantly based on several factors including the complexity of the case, the cooperation of both parties, the court's docket, and even unforeseen circumstances. It could take a few months, or even longer. Patience and persistence are needed, while regular communication with your legal counsel will keep you informed.

Remember, obtaining a modification isn't guaranteed. The court will only grant a modification if the presented evidence convincingly demonstrates a significant and material change in circumstances. The burden of proof rests with the party seeking the modification. A well-prepared and strategically presented case increases your chances of success.

Finally, consider the emotional toll. Modifying a spousal support order can be emotionally challenging, frequently leading to stress and anxiety. Maintaining open communication with your attorney and potentially utilizing support networks are vital to navigate this process. Remember to take care of your mental well-being throughout this time, as your emotional resilience will contribute to your overall success. You're not going through this alone.

5.3 Termination of Support

Spousal support, or alimony, often ends, but the circumstances surrounding termination are varied and complex. Understanding these conditions is crucial for both parties involved, protecting their rights and financial well-being. It's not simply a matter of a set date; several factors could bring an end to these payments, some planned and some unexpected.

A common way spousal support ends is upon the expiration of a predetermined time frame. The divorce decree usually specifies a duration – it might be a specific number of years, or it might be tied to a certain event, like the recipient's completion of education or the attainment of gainful employment. Careful review of the legal document is essential; overlooking a key date can lead to unforeseen legal complications. Always consult with your legal counsel to clarify any ambiguities within the agreement.

Conversely, the termination might hinge on the recipient's remarriage. Many decrees stipulate that spousal support ceases immediately upon the supported spouse entering a new marriage. This is a legally recognized trigger event, often included to reflect the shift in financial circumstances and responsibilities. However, cohabitation, while sometimes viewed similarly, isn't automatically considered equivalent to marriage, depending on the specifics of the agreement. These nuances demand careful legal interpretation. Consult your lawyer to understand how this specific clause applies to your situation.

Death, naturally, terminates support payments from both sides of the equation. The death of either the payer or the recipient renders the support agreement void. This is straightforward, a finality inherent in the nature of the event. While seemingly uncomplicated, verifying the death certificate and filing the necessary paperwork with the court ensures the official conclusion of the spousal support obligation. Never assume this step is unnecessary – proper documentation is always vital.

Significant changes in the supported spouse's financial situation can also lead to a modification or termination of support. A substantial increase in income, for example, may justify a reduction or cessation of payments, as the original rationale for support – a significant disparity in income – no longer applies. Conversely, an unexpected downturn in the payer's financial standing can trigger a court review of the support amount, potentially reducing the payments. Such changes demand careful documentation and legal action; petitioning the court for modification is the appropriate legal channel.

Furthermore, the supported spouse's cohabitation with a new partner could result in a reduction or termination of alimony. While not automatically considered equivalent to remarriage in all jurisdictions, long-term, financially interdependent relationships can be viewed by the court as a relevant factor in assessing the ongoing need for spousal support. This is frequently a point of contention, demanding a thorough understanding of case law and local legal precedents to build a robust argument. Your legal advisor can guide you through the complexities and present a strong case.

The termination of spousal support isn't a monolithic process.

It's a multifaceted area governed by specific state laws and the terms of the divorce decree. Failing to understand these nuances can have significant consequences. Ignoring the possibility of changes, or failing to proactively seek a modification, can leave one party vulnerable to significant financial hardship. Therefore, open communication and regular legal counsel are vital to both navigating the complexities of spousal support and avoiding potential pitfalls. Clear communication between both parties is also helpful.

Ignoring the terms of the agreement can have legal consequences, so careful reading and understanding of the decree are vital. The implications of breach of contract are severe, potentially leading to further legal action and financial penalties. A proactive approach, involving regular review and consultation with legal professionals, is the most effective way to ensure compliance and avoid costly mistakes. This is particularly true when facing unexpected changes or new circumstances.

In conclusion, the termination of spousal support isn't a simple event defined by a single date. It's a legally complex process influenced by several factors, including time constraints, remarriage, death, and substantial financial changes in either party's life. Understanding these facets is critical for safeguarding your rights and financial future. Consulting an experienced family law attorney provides the necessary guidance, ensuring a smooth, legally sound process throughout. Remember: Proactive legal counsel is crucial, ensuring a clear understanding of your rights and responsibilities concerning spousal support and its termination. Don't hesitate to seek professional help; it can make all the difference. The advice of a legal expert is invaluable when navigating these often complicated and emotionally charged situations. Finally, carefully review all relevant legal documents and ensure a thorough comprehension of all clauses and their implications.

6 Chapter 6: Negotiation & Mediation

Many divorces become protracted battles, filled with animosity and escalating legal fees. However, alternative dispute resolution methods, specifically negotiation and mediation, offer a less adversarial path toward resolution. Choosing this route can significantly reduce stress, preserve relationships (where possible), and ultimately, save considerable financial resources.

Successful negotiation requires thoughtful preparation. Before engaging with your spouse or their attorney, meticulously gather all relevant financial documents: bank statements, tax returns, retirement account statements, property deeds, and any other records pertaining to assets and debts. A clear understanding of your financial picture empowers you to negotiate effectively and convincingly. Remember to prioritize your non-negotiables—those aspects you absolutely refuse to compromise on—while remaining flexible on less crucial points.

Mediation, a more structured approach, involves a neutral third party, a mediator, facilitating communication between you and your spouse. The mediator doesn't offer legal advice, but guides the discussion, helping you reach a mutually acceptable agreement. This process requires active listening and a willingness to compromise. While initially daunting, it can be remarkably effective in fostering collaboration and reducing the emotional toll of litigation. The mediator's role is to keep the conversation focused and productive, helping both sides to understand each other's perspectives.

One of the significant benefits of mediation is the increased control you maintain over the outcome. Unlike a court decision, which is entirely outside your hands, mediation allows you to actively participate in shaping the terms of your divorce settlement. This empowers you to create a resolution tailored to your specific needs and circumstances, a significant advantage compared to the rigid structure of a courtroom. Moreover, mediation fosters a sense of ownership and accountability, ensuring both parties feel heard and respected throughout the process.

However, mediation isn't a panacea. It's crucial to understand its limitations. Mediation is only effective when both parties are genuinely committed to resolving their differences amicably. If one party is unwilling to participate constructively or engages in bad faith tactics, mediation is likely to fail. Similarly, mediation may not be suitable in cases involving domestic violence, substance abuse, or significant power imbalances. In such situations, a more formal legal process might be necessary to ensure the safety and well-being of involved parties. Careful consideration of your unique circumstances is vital to determine the suitability of mediation.

Collaborative divorce is a more recent alternative that shares many similarities with mediation, but with added structure. This method often involves multiple professionals working together—lawyers, financial advisors, and possibly mental health professionals—to assist couples in crafting a comprehensive agreement. Each party retains their own attorney, but the attorneys commit to resolving the issues constructively without resorting to litigation. The collaborative process emphasizes open communication, cooperation, and the preservation of relationships, even after the separation is complete. It requires a commitment from both parties to cooperate and focus on problem-solving.

Effective negotiation and mediation require more than just good intentions; they demand careful planning and a clear understanding of your legal rights and responsibilities. Consider seeking the advice of an experienced family law attorney before initiating negotiations or mediation. They can help you assess the strengths and weaknesses of your case, clarify your legal options, and assist you in developing a comprehensive strategy to protect your interests. While many resources are available online, you need tailored professional guidance to navigate these sensitive matters. A lawyer's expertise ensures you're equipped to navigate the complex legal landscape and secure the best possible outcome in your situation.

Remember that the goal of negotiation and mediation is not simply to end the divorce proceedings as quickly as possible, but rather to reach a fair and equitable settlement that addresses the needs and concerns of all parties involved. A well-negotiated agreement can offer a far more satisfying conclusion than a court-ordered resolution, fostering peace of mind and stability as you transition into the next chapter of your life. Therefore, taking the time to understand these processes and to prepare thoroughly will significantly contribute to a more positive resolution. This proactive approach can lead to a more balanced and sustainable outcome for both parties.

6.1 Negotiation Strategies

Effective negotiation hinges on preparation. Before you even sit down with your spouse or their attorney, meticulously gather all relevant financial documents. This includes bank statements, tax returns, investment records, property deeds, and any documentation related to debts. A thorough understanding of your combined assets and liabilities is paramount; without it, you're negotiating blindfolded. Remember, precision matters—accurate figures prevent future disputes and ensure a fair settlement. Ignoring this crucial step can leave you vulnerable to unfavorable terms. Consider consulting a financial advisor to independently assess your financial situation and develop a realistic strategy. This independent perspective can provide a vital counterbalance to the emotional complexities of divorce.

Know your "bottom line," your non-negotiable positions. What are the absolute minimum acceptable outcomes for you regarding property division, child custody, and spousal support? Defining these limits in advance prevents emotional decisions during the negotiation process. It gives you a clear framework to evaluate offers and prevents you from accepting something less than you deserve. Conversely, understanding your spouse's likely priorities can give you leverage. Knowing their potential needs or vulnerabilities can inform your negotiation tactics. It's not about exploiting weakness, but about understanding the dynamics at play to find a mutually acceptable solution.

Effective communication is the cornerstone of successful negotiation. Active listening—truly hearing and understanding your spouse's perspective—is crucial. Avoid interrupting or becoming defensive; instead, focus on creating a dialogue. Frame your statements collaboratively, using "we" language to foster a sense of partnership. Remember, the goal is a resolution, not a victory. Strive to find common ground, even on seemingly irreconcilable issues. Employ empathy, even when challenging, understanding that the divorce process is painful for everyone involved. Emphasize your shared goals, like ensuring the well-being of your children or maintaining a civil relationship post-divorce.

Consider your communication style. Are you direct and assertive, or more indirect and conciliatory? Adapting your approach based on your spouse's style can greatly enhance communication. If your spouse is emotional, try a more patient and understanding approach. If they are logical and analytical, present your case with well-supported arguments and data. Avoid accusatory language or personal attacks. Focus on facts and figures, avoiding emotional outbursts that will only hinder progress. This level-headed approach will create space for rational compromise. Remember, respectful communication is key to achieving an equitable settlement.

Compromise is inevitable. Negotiation is rarely a win-win scenario in the traditional sense. However, by focusing on mutual interests and creating solutions that meet most of each party's needs, you can achieve a settlement that's acceptable to both parties. Be willing to concede on less important issues to secure favorable terms on more significant ones. It's about strategic concessions, not giving up everything. Remember that a truly successful negotiation is one that results in an agreement both parties are content to live with. This approach can reduce the need for lengthy and expensive legal battles.

Document everything. Keep a detailed record of all communication, proposals, agreements, and compromises. This meticulous record-keeping protects you should disagreements arise. Precise documentation ensures you have evidence to support your claims should the need arise. It's far better to have comprehensive documentation than to rely on memory, especially during such an emotionally charged period. This documentation is critical for potential future issues and provides a vital record of your progress through the negotiations. Consider using a digital platform to facilitate this process and ensure easy access to all documents.

Know when to seek professional help. Even with meticulous preparation, some situations require outside expertise. A mediator can help facilitate communication and guide you through the negotiation process. While mediating your divorce doesn't guarantee a specific result, it provides a structured approach and often leads to quicker, less costly settlements. If negotiations repeatedly fail or become overly hostile, your legal representation can provide counsel and advice, protecting your legal rights and representing your best interests within the legal framework.

Ultimately, effective negotiation in divorce requires a strategic blend of preparation, communication, and a willingness to compromise. By following these strategies, you can significantly increase your chances of reaching a mutually acceptable settlement, minimizing conflict and ultimately, helping you move towards a more peaceful future. Remember, while the process is challenging, focusing on a practical and equitable outcome, rather than seeking vengeance, often leads to a more sustainable solution for everyone involved. The long-term implications of the agreements you reach now extend far beyond the immediate resolution of your divorce.

6.2 Mediation Process

The mediation process offers a structured, less adversarial approach to resolving divorce disputes. It's a facilitated negotiation where a neutral third party, the mediator, guides you and your spouse toward a mutually agreeable settlement. Unlike a courtroom setting, mediation emphasizes collaboration and problem-solving. This collaborative spirit fosters a more productive environment, reducing the emotional toll often associated with traditional litigation. The mediator doesn't impose solutions; instead, they facilitate open communication, helping you identify common ground and explore creative solutions that address everyone's concerns. This process is particularly beneficial when dealing with complex issues like child custody arrangements and property division, where finding a solution that serves the best interests of all parties involved is paramount. The mediator's role extends to helping you clarify your positions, consider alternative options, and create a legally sound agreement that reflects your priorities. Remember, the goal is not simply to reach an agreement, but to reach an agreement you both feel is fair and equitable.

Unlike court battles that can become lengthy and expensive, mediation provides a quicker and often less costly resolution. Time constraints that accompany litigation simply don't exist. You control the pace of your negotiations. This allows for more thoughtful consideration of your options and a greater degree of participation in crafting the terms of your settlement, rather than having a judge impose a decision upon you. The cost savings are substantial, as mediation fees are typically far lower than legal fees associated with court proceedings. And, you don't have to worry about the unpredictable expenses that can arise during protracted litigation. Mediation offers predictable costs and a manageable timeline, making it a more financially responsible alternative.

However, mediation isn't always the perfect solution. Its success hinges on the willingness of both parties to participate actively and in good faith. If one party is unwilling to compromise or engage constructively, the process may be unproductive. Furthermore, mediation may not be appropriate in cases involving domestic violence, substance abuse, or significant power imbalances where one party might feel pressured to accept an unfair settlement. In such situations, it's essential to prioritize your safety and seek legal counsel to protect your rights. Your lawyer can assess the suitability of mediation given the specific circumstances of your case. They can offer valuable advice to ensure you are making informed decisions and navigating the process effectively.

Effective preparation is crucial for a successful mediation. You need to carefully gather all relevant financial documents, including bank statements, tax returns, and property appraisals. Organize these documents logically for easy access. Also, take time to clearly articulate your goals and priorities. What are your non-negotiables? What areas are you more flexible on? Consider these issues carefully beforehand and formulate your preferred solutions. This is crucial so that you can effectively communicate your needs to the mediator and your spouse. It's imperative that you understand your rights and the legal implications of any agreement you might reach during the mediation process.

Remember, the mediator is there to facilitate the process, not to represent your interests. You should still have your own attorney review any proposed settlement agreement before signing it.

This ensures that the agreement is legally sound, protects your rights, and accurately reflects what you agreed upon. This step safeguards against potential future legal disputes and ensures you have comprehensive legal protection throughout this sensitive phase. Your attorney can provide an independent legal perspective and advise you on whether the settlement terms are fair and equitable within the context of applicable laws. While the conciliatory atmosphere of mediation promotes amicable resolution, it's crucial to maintain a legal perspective on the proceedings.
Mediation, therefore, is a powerful tool but it's not a universal fix. It's a highly personalized process requiring careful consideration and preparation, not just on your part, but also the participation and willingness of your ex-spouse. Its success depends greatly on the parties' commitment to finding a mutually acceptable resolution. Weigh the pros and cons carefully, considering your specific situation and the involvement of all relevant parties. This decision-making process requires an honest assessment of your circumstances, a realistic expectation of the outcome, and a clear understanding of the role of the mediator and your own legal representation. Your personal comfort level and the willingness of the other party are equally paramount, since ultimately, mediation works best when everyone walks away feeling heard and reasonably satisfied.

6.3 Benefits of Mediation

Reduced stress and emotional toll are significant benefits. The adversarial nature of court proceedings often exacerbates conflict, leading to heightened anxiety and emotional distress for all involved. Mediation, however, provides a structured environment focused on collaboration and compromise, thereby minimizing emotional strain and fostering a more constructive resolution. This gentler approach can be particularly crucial when children are involved, safeguarding their well-being amidst parental conflict. The reduced emotional burden allows individuals to focus on rebuilding their lives more effectively following the separation. This peaceful resolution can translate to a faster recovery and improved mental health outcomes.

Cost savings are substantial. Legal battles can be incredibly expensive, involving hefty attorney fees, court costs, and protracted legal processes. Mediation significantly reduces these costs. The streamlined process and reduced need for extensive legal representation contribute to significant financial savings, making it an attractive and financially responsible alternative, especially beneficial for those with limited resources or facing financial hardship during the already taxing process of divorce. These savings can then be reinvested into other priorities as the individuals begin a new chapter in their lives.

Increased control and flexibility are key advantages. Court proceedings often leave individuals feeling powerless, subject to a judge's decisions with limited input on the final outcome. Mediation empowers participants by giving them direct control over the resolution. They actively shape the terms of their settlement, tailoring it to their specific needs and circumstances. This participatory approach enhances a sense of ownership and satisfaction with the outcome, fostering greater acceptance and reducing resentment. The flexibility of mediation also allows for creative solutions that may not be possible within the rigid framework of traditional litigation.

Preservation of relationships is a noteworthy benefit. The confrontational nature of court can severely damage relationships, not only between spouses but also among extended family members. Mediation prioritizes maintaining respectful communication, encouraging dialogue and cooperation to reach a mutually acceptable agreement. This approach preserves dignity and allows for a more amicable parting, fostering healthier relationships moving forward. This is especially valuable for preserving relationships with children, minimizing the negative impact of parental conflict. The emphasis on collaboration often allows for a more civil co-parenting relationship post-divorce, promoting the well-being of the children involved.

Faster resolution times are a significant advantage over protracted litigation. Court cases can drag on for months or even years, creating uncertainty and prolonging emotional distress. Mediation offers a significantly faster resolution process. The collaborative nature and focused approach often lead to settlements within a shorter timeframe, providing much-needed closure and enabling individuals to move forward with their lives more swiftly. This expeditious resolution is extremely beneficial, minimizing the disruption to the lives of everyone involved. The reduced waiting period facilitates a quicker transition and a faster start on rebuilding lives.

Confidential settlements are achieved in mediation. Court proceedings are public record, which can have long-term implications for individuals involved. Mediation, however, allows for confidential settlements, protecting personal details and ensuring privacy. This protection is particularly crucial in instances where sensitive financial or personal information is involved. Confidentiality promotes a more open and honest dialogue, encouraging participants to share relevant information freely without fear of public exposure. Maintaining confidentiality during and after the mediation contributes to a sense of dignity and closure. It allows for a more graceful transition, minimizing unnecessary public scrutiny.

A more creative solution is possible through mediation. Court-ordered solutions are often bound by strict legal precedent, potentially limiting the scope of creative solutions. Mediation allows for greater flexibility, allowing the parties to explore diverse options and craft a unique resolution tailored to their specific circumstances. This freedom from strict legal constraints often leads to more innovative and mutually beneficial outcomes, addressing unique aspects of the divorce that might not be accommodated by a standard court order. This flexibility is especially important when dealing with complex asset divisions or unique family situations.

Finally, mediation fosters a greater sense of self-determination. Unlike the courtroom where a judge ultimately decides the outcome, mediation places the power of resolution directly in the hands of the separating couple. This increased control leads to a greater sense of empowerment and acceptance of the final agreement. This sense of ownership often translates to greater compliance with the terms of the agreement and reduces the likelihood of future disputes. Self-determination empowers individuals to take responsibility for their future and enables them to rebuild their lives on their own terms.

6.4 Limitations of Mediation

Mediation, while often touted as a less adversarial and more cost-effective alternative to traditional litigation, possesses inherent limitations that prospective participants should carefully consider. It relies heavily on the willingness of both parties to engage in good-faith negotiation and compromise, a prerequisite often absent in deeply entrenched conflicts marked by significant emotional distress or mistrust. The success of mediation hinges on a collaborative spirit, which may be unrealistic in cases involving abuse, extensive financial disputes, or fundamental disagreements about child custody arrangements.

Unlike court proceedings where a judge ultimately renders a decision, mediation lacks the power of legal enforcement. While a mediated agreement carries considerable weight, its enforceability depends entirely on the parties' adherence to the terms. If one party subsequently reneges on the agreement, returning to court to enforce it becomes necessary, potentially negating the initial time and cost savings. This potential for non-compliance necessitates a thorough understanding of the agreement's enforceability and the subsequent legal recourse available should the agreement fail. The process itself lacks the formality and structure of a courtroom, potentially leaving some participants feeling uncertain about its legal implications.

Power imbalances between spouses can significantly hinder the effectiveness of mediation. If one party possesses significantly greater financial resources or legal acumen, they might exert undue influence during the negotiation process, leading to an unfair settlement. This imbalance can be particularly problematic in cases where one spouse is economically dependent on the other or lacks the capacity to fully grasp the complex financial or legal aspects of the case. Such scenarios demonstrate the need for independent legal counsel even within the mediation process to ensure a fair outcome. This ensures that all participants are on level ground in navigating the complexities and ensuring their interests are adequately protected. This is even more crucial in situations where substantial assets are involved, requiring professional assessments and valuations.

Furthermore, mediation may not be suitable for all types of cases. Cases involving complex financial matters, extensive assets, or allegations of domestic violence often necessitate the more structured and legally binding framework of court proceedings. The complexities of dividing intricate business interests, evaluating the value of closely held corporations, or determining the appropriate level of child support in high-income situations often exceed the capabilities of a mediator to resolve effectively. This underscores the limitations of mediation in situations demanding precise legal interpretation and a judge's final decision regarding highly specialized financial issues, like those related to closely held company valuations, where specialized financial expertise may be needed for accurate assessments.

The process also demands a considerable investment of time and emotional energy from both parties. Multiple mediation sessions may be required to reach an agreement, extending the overall duration of the divorce process. This can be particularly burdensome for individuals already facing emotional distress, which can further complicate the negotiation process and hinder the chances of achieving a mutually agreeable settlement. A realistic expectation of time and energy commitment is essential for parties considering mediation as a means of resolving their divorce-related issues. Such preparation may involve seeking emotional support or guidance from therapists and counselors to ensure participants navigate the emotional challenges effectively and are well-prepared to engage constructively in the mediation process.

Finally, mediators, while skilled negotiators, aren't judges. They cannot impose solutions, leaving the final resolution entirely dependent upon the parties' willingness to compromise. If agreement remains elusive, the parties are left to pursue more adversarial legal routes. This possibility underscores the need to carefully consider the potential for the mediation process to fail, leaving the parties in a potentially worse position than before beginning the mediation attempt. In such cases, the time and expense incurred during the mediation process may prove detrimental, highlighting the crucial importance of considering potential alternatives and having a realistic contingency plan in place before embarking on the mediation process. The lack of judicial authority means the process is inherently reliant on both parties' willingness to negotiate in good faith and find common ground, a factor that cannot be guaranteed.

6.5 Collaborative Divorce

Collaborative divorce offers a unique path, diverging from the adversarial nature of traditional divorce proceedings. It's a process built on cooperation, where both spouses commit to working together, guided by their respective lawyers, towards a mutually agreeable settlement. This approach prioritizes open communication and shared decision-making, fostering a more respectful and less contentious environment, especially beneficial when children are involved. Unlike mediation, where a neutral third party facilitates discussions, collaborative divorce actively involves the attorneys as integral participants in the negotiation process. They play a crucial role in guiding the couple, ensuring the agreement is legally sound and comprehensively addresses all relevant issues.

The collaborative process typically begins with an agreement between both parties to participate wholeheartedly. This commitment necessitates a willingness to disclose all relevant information openly and honestly, building a foundation of trust necessary for effective negotiation. Each spouse retains their own attorney, yet these lawyers are specifically trained in collaborative law principles. Their role extends beyond mere legal representation; they actively assist in facilitating productive conversations, identifying potential obstacles, and creatively crafting solutions that meet both parties' needs. The collaborative spirit extends to all participants, fostering an atmosphere of mutual respect and understanding. This collaborative approach minimizes emotional distress, making the transition less jarring and more manageable for all involved, particularly for the children who may be impacted most profoundly by the divorce.

A key component of collaborative divorce is the focus on interest-based negotiation. Unlike positional bargaining, which involves rigidly adhering to initial demands, interest-based negotiation seeks to understand the underlying needs and interests driving each party's position. This requires open dialogue, empathy, and a willingness to explore creative solutions that address those fundamental needs. For example, instead of fighting over the marital home, a collaborative approach might involve exploring options such as temporary usage rights or a flexible payment plan that helps both parties transition smoothly. The ability to explore creative options is essential. The process encourages flexibility and a willingness to find compromises that satisfy each spouse's needs. This often results in more creative solutions than those possible in a courtroom setting where rigid legal arguments can restrict options.

Financial transparency is a cornerstone of successful collaborative divorce. This entails a thorough and honest disclosure of all assets, liabilities, and income. Detailed financial statements prepared by a neutral financial professional can streamline this process, providing a common understanding of the couple's financial picture. This transparency ensures both parties have a clear view of the resources available for division and makes it easier to negotiate a fair and equitable settlement. It can significantly reduce the likelihood of disputes arising from a lack of information or perceived unfairness in the distribution of assets. This is crucial in minimizing the time, cost, and emotional toll associated with the divorce process.

Children are always a central consideration in collaborative divorce, especially when determining custody and visitation schedules. The collaborative process fosters a child-centered approach. Discussions revolve around what is in the best interests of the child and how the parents can work together to create a stable and nurturing environment for them, regardless of their own relationship. This involves creating a child-focused plan that helps them adapt and cope with the changes resulting from the divorce. This can take the form of collaborative parenting plans that encourage co-parenting arrangements and clearly define responsibilities. It also often includes professional advice from child psychologists or therapists to ensure children's needs are adequately addressed throughout the process.

However, it's important to acknowledge that collaborative divorce isn't a perfect solution for every couple. It requires a certain level of mutual respect, trust, and willingness to compromise. If either spouse is unwilling to engage in good faith or if significant power imbalances exist, collaborative divorce may not be the most appropriate approach. In such cases, traditional litigation or mediation might be more suitable. The process works best when both parties are committed to finding a solution outside the courtroom and have faith that the process will result in a fair and equitable outcome. The collaborative process can be a valuable tool for those willing to invest in a process that prioritizes cooperation and mutual respect.

7 Chapter 7: Final Orders & Enforcement

The final decree, that official document signifying the legal end of your marriage, isn't just paperwork; it's the culmination of a potentially lengthy and emotionally draining process. Securing this decree requires careful attention to detail and a thorough understanding of the court's requirements. Remember, even after signing, the implications of the decree extend far beyond the courtroom, impacting your finances, your children, and your future. Understanding these implications is paramount to successful navigation of the post-divorce landscape. Ignoring this stage can lead to future complications, even legal battles, that could have been avoided with careful attention to the finalization process.

Obtaining the final decree often involves a final hearing, providing one last opportunity to address any outstanding issues. Be prepared; it's not uncommon for previously agreed-upon terms to require minor adjustments or clarifications during this stage. This is a chance to confirm every detail, ensuring accuracy and preventing future disputes. This is your chance to ensure all aspects of your divorce settlement – child custody, spousal support, asset division – are clearly and precisely reflected in the court's ruling. Bring all your documents and be ready to answer questions from the judge.

Sometimes, circumstances change significantly after the divorce is finalized. Perhaps you've experienced a major job loss, or a substantial change in your child's needs. In such cases, modifying court orders becomes necessary. This process isn't as simple as sending a letter. It requires filing a formal motion with the court, providing compelling evidence of the changed circumstances. This is not something to take lightly. The court will closely scrutinize your reasons, ensuring that the changes are justified and impact the original agreements. Simply wanting a change isn't enough; it necessitates a significant alteration of your personal circumstances affecting the factors considered in the original divorce order.

Modifying custody arrangements, for instance, requires demonstrating a substantial change in the child's best interests. This could involve a change in the child's school, significant changes in the parents' living situations, or serious concerns about the child's welfare. The burden of proof lies with the party seeking the modification; clear and convincing evidence is crucial for a successful petition. This involves meticulous documentation: medical records, school reports, even personal journals detailing significant events may be needed as proof. Without robust evidence, your petition might be dismissed.

Modifying spousal support orders, equally challenging, necessitates demonstrating a material change in the financial circumstances of either party. This isn't a slight income fluctuation; rather, it requires a significant event like a job loss, a disability, or a substantial increase in medical expenses. Again, thorough documentation is key. Financial statements, tax returns, and bank statements must substantiate your claims. The court seeks to ensure fairness and will examine these documents carefully before altering the pre-existing agreement.

Enforcement of court orders is another critical aspect of this final stage. If your ex-spouse fails to comply with the agreed-upon terms— whether concerning child support, property division, or visitation rights— you must take action. This might involve filing a motion for contempt of court. Such motions trigger a court hearing where noncompliance is addressed. The court possesses the power to enforce compliance, through fines, wage garnishment, or even imprisonment in extreme cases. Non-compliance can lead to a cycle of legal battles, making proactive engagement crucial to maintaining the order's integrity.

Remember, the legal system isn't designed to be navigated alone. Throughout this process, consulting with your attorney remains crucial. They can guide you through the complexities of modifying orders or enforcing compliance, ensuring you understand your rights and options. They will help you prepare the necessary documentation, strategize your approach, and represent you in court, potentially saving you significant time, money, and stress. Their expertise is invaluable in these crucial stages. Consider them your advocate during this delicate time. Failing to seek professional legal counsel at this juncture could lead to costly and potentially devastating outcomes. Therefore, remember to stay informed, organized and proactive throughout the process.

7.1 Entering a Final Decree

The final decree represents the culmination of a lengthy and often emotionally draining process. It's the official legal document that legally dissolves your marriage, solidifying the agreements reached regarding child custody, spousal support, and the division of marital assets. Think of it as the period at the end of a very long sentence—a sentence filled with stress, negotiation, and legal maneuvering. Receiving this decree marks a significant milestone, even if the path leading to it wasn't exactly straightforward. This isn't simply a piece of paper; it's the official end to a chapter of your life.

Understanding the implications of this document is crucial. It isn't just about the ending; it's about the beginning of a new phase. The decree details specific legal obligations and responsibilities, determining factors such as child visitation schedules, financial contributions, and property ownership. Failure to fully comprehend its contents can lead to future legal complications, potentially requiring further court intervention and incurring additional legal expenses. Take your time; read it meticulously.

Your lawyer should thoroughly explain each section of the decree. Don't hesitate to ask questions, no matter how seemingly insignificant they may appear. A clear understanding of the terms is paramount. Many people, overwhelmed by the entire process, gloss over details. This is a mistake. Make sure you understand every aspect, from the precise wording of the custody arrangement to the exact figures related to financial obligations. Remember, you are legally bound by this document, so clarity is absolutely essential. Ignorance is not an excuse for non-compliance.

Remember the arduous journey that preceded this moment.

You've likely navigated complex negotiations, possibly mediation, and potentially even contentious court hearings. The final decree is the tangible result of all that effort. This official document formalizes every agreement you made, from the smallest detail regarding personal possessions to the most significant decisions involving your children's well-being. It's a testament to your resilience and your capacity to navigate a challenging legal landscape.

Once you have the decree in hand, it's vital to keep a copy in a safe and readily accessible place. Many prefer to have both digital and hard copies, just in case. Additionally, review it periodically, especially if significant life changes occur. While modifications are possible under certain circumstances, they aren't easily obtained and typically require demonstrating a substantial change in circumstances. This could include a job loss, a major illness, or a significant change in a child's needs. These aren't things you want to deal with without a clear understanding of your rights and your ex-spouse's rights as outlined in the decree.

Consider the emotional weight of this moment. The final decree is more than just a legal document; it often represents a major turning point in your life. It can bring a sense of closure, but also perhaps a mix of other emotions. While the legal proceedings are concluded, processing the emotional aftermath of a divorce is an ongoing process. Seeking support from friends, family, therapists, or support groups can be profoundly beneficial. Don't hesitate to use available resources to help you transition into this new phase of your life. Remember, navigating this emotionally charged period shouldn't be done alone.

The signing of the final decree doesn't signify the end of your responsibilities or obligations. It simply marks a shift in how those responsibilities and obligations are managed. Maintaining open communication, adhering to the terms of the decree, and keeping accurate records are crucial for navigating the post-divorce landscape. This includes diligently documenting financial transactions, especially regarding child support and spousal support payments. Maintaining clear records ensures transparency and minimizes potential future disputes. Proactive record-keeping is paramount to avoiding future conflicts and ensuring that the terms of the agreement are being upheld.

In conclusion, the final decree isn't just the end of a legal process; it's the beginning of a new chapter. It's a formalization of agreements carefully considered and negotiated, often after considerable emotional turmoil and legal maneuvering. Fully understanding its contents and maintaining meticulous records are essential for a smooth transition into your post-divorce life. Remember the journey that brought you here, and remember the tools and resources available to help you navigate what lies ahead. The legal aspect of divorce is over; however, remember this is a beginning, not an end. The process of rebuilding your life starts now.

7.2 Modifying Court Orders

Life rarely stands still, and neither do circumstances. A final divorce decree, while seemingly conclusive, might require adjustments as life unfolds. Unexpected job loss, a significant illness, or a child's evolving needs—these are just some of the events that could necessitate modifying a court order. Understanding the process is crucial to navigating these unexpected turns.

Successfully modifying a court order hinges on demonstrating a substantial and material change in circumstances since the original order was issued. This isn't merely a matter of minor inconveniences; it demands a significant shift impacting the original agreement's foundation. For instance, a slight pay cut might not suffice, but a prolonged period of unemployment, leading to demonstrable financial hardship, certainly could. Similarly, a child's diagnosed illness requiring extensive and costly treatment would likely qualify as a material change affecting child support or custody arrangements. Precisely defining "substantial" and "material" often requires legal counsel.

Gathering comprehensive and verifiable documentation is paramount. This isn't about hearsay or personal opinions; you need concrete evidence to support your request. Pay stubs, medical records, tax returns, and bank statements can substantiate claims of financial hardship or changed needs. If seeking a modification related to child custody, documentation supporting a child's well-being or educational needs becomes essential. Thorough documentation strengthens your case significantly.

The method for modifying a court order varies depending on the jurisdiction and the specific aspect being modified. In some jurisdictions, a simple motion might suffice, particularly for minor modifications. However, more complex changes, such as significant custody alterations or substantial child support adjustments, often necessitate formal legal proceedings. You may need to file a new motion with the court, outlining the reasons for the modification request, presenting evidence, and possibly appearing before a judge. Understanding your local rules of court is vital.

Navigating the legal complexities alone can be daunting, even for seasoned professionals. Legal counsel provides indispensable guidance throughout this process. An attorney can assist with drafting the necessary legal documents, representing you in court, and ensuring you adhere to all procedural rules. Their expertise proves invaluable in building a strong case and successfully navigating the intricacies of the legal system. Remember, seeking legal advice doesn't indicate weakness; rather, it underscores a proactive and informed approach.

The legal timeline for modifying a court order isn't fixed; it's highly dependent on various factors, including court congestion, the complexity of the case, and the willingness of all parties involved to cooperate. In some instances, modifications might be reached swiftly and amicably through negotiation or mediation. Other times, extensive legal battles might ensue, significantly extending the process. Patience and realistic expectations are crucial as you navigate this phase.

While modifications are possible, they aren't guaranteed. The court will assess the presented evidence to determine if the requested changes are warranted and in the best interests of all involved, particularly children. A judge will consider the original order's context, the stated reasons for modification, the presented evidence, and the overall impact on everyone affected. Understanding the court's perspective and building a compelling case is critical to achieving a favorable outcome.

Finally, remember that modifying a court order is not a casual process. It requires careful preparation, sound legal strategy, and the ability to present a strong and convincing argument. While unexpected changes in life are inevitable, understanding the procedures for modifying court orders empowers you to address these changes with confidence and clarity. Thorough preparation, strong documentation, and skilled legal representation are the cornerstones of a successful modification. The process can feel overwhelming; however, preparation and legal support can significantly ease the burden and increase the chances of a positive resolution.